MW00411728

this Book Belongs to:

_____

Dance school:

_____

And the merry love the fiddle,
And the merry love to dance.
~ *William Butler Yeats*

Copyright © 2011, 2015, 2017, 2019, 2023

feisBooks

All rights reserved

íRísh ɒaɒce feís ReCORɒ BOOk

- Feisbooks provide a convenient place to keep track of feis results, apparel purchases, travel notes and more.

- There are enough pages to record the results of 45 feiseanna, plus notes, apparel records, travel notes and an Ireland map.

- The handy 6 x 9 inch size fits in purses and dance bags.

- They make the perfect accessory and gift for the Irish dancer in your life.

- Feisbooks have been sold worldwide since 2001.

- Feisbooks also sells Irish Dance Word Searches and other fun activity books for Irish dancers.

Feis Record Books are available in two styles:
- Grades Level (Beginner/Novice/Prizewinner)
- Champion Level (Preliminary/Open)

Record of Apparel
(size, vendor, date, comments)

soft shoes:

hard shoes:

socks/tights:

class costume:

solo costume:

wig/tiara:

boy tie/belt:

accessories:

Record of Apparel
(size, vendor, date, comments)

soft shoes:

hard shoes:

socks/tights:

class costume:

solo costume:

wig/tiara:

boy tie/belt:

accessories:

RECORO OF APPARel
(size, vendor, date, comments)

soft shoes:

haro shoes:

socks/tights:

class costume:

solo costume:

wig/tiara:

Boy tie/Belt:

accessories:

Notes:

Feis Name: _____

Date: Location: Dancer #:

COMPETITION	LEVEL/AGE	# DANCERS	COMMENTS	RESULTS
Reel				
Light Jig				
Slip Jig				
Single Jig				
Treble Jig				
Hornpipe				
Traditional Set				

SPECIALS	LEVEL/AGE	# DANCERS	COMMENTS	RESULTS

TEAMS	LEVEL/AGE	# TEAMS	COMMENTS	RESULTS

Notes:

Feis Name: _____

Date: *Location:*   *Dancer #:*

COMPETITION	LEVEL/AGE	# DANCERS	COMMENTS	RESULTS
Reel				
Light Jig				
Slip Jig				
Single Jig				
Treble Jig				
Hornpipe				
Traditional Set				

SPECIALS	LEVEL/AGE	# DANCERS	COMMENTS	RESULTS

TEAMS	LEVEL/AGE	# TEAMS	COMMENTS	RESULTS

Notes:

Feis Name: _____

Date: Location: Dancer #:

COMPETITION	LEVEL/AGE	# DANCERS	COMMENTS	RESULTS
Reel				
Light Jig				
Slip Jig				
Single Jig				
Treble Jig				
Hornpipe				
Traditional Set				

SPECIALS	LEVEL/AGE	# DANCERS	COMMENTS	RESULTS

TEAMS	LEVEL/AGE	# TEAMS	COMMENTS	RESULTS

Notes:

Feis Name: _____

Date: *Location:*   *Dancer #:*

COMPETITION	LEVEL/AGE	# DANCERS	COMMENTS	RESULTS
Reel				
Light Jig				
Slip Jig				
Single Jig				
Treble Jig				
Hornpipe				
Traditional Set				

SPECIALS	LEVEL/AGE	# DANCERS	COMMENTS	RESULTS

TEAMS	LEVEL/AGE	# TEAMS	COMMENTS	RESULTS

Notes:

Feis Name: _____

Date: Location: Dancer #:

COMPETITION	LEVEL/AGE	# DANCERS	COMMENTS	RESULTS
Reel				
Light Jig				
Slip Jig				
Single Jig				
Treble Jig				
Hornpipe				
Traditional Set				

SPECIALS	LEVEL/AGE	# DANCERS	COMMENTS	RESULTS

TEAMS	LEVEL/AGE	# TEAMS	COMMENTS	RESULTS

Notes:

Feis Name: _____

Date: Location: Dancer #:

COMPETITION	LEVEL/AGE	# DANCERS	COMMENTS	RESULTS
Reel				
Light Jig				
Slip Jig				
Single Jig				
Treble Jig				
Hornpipe				
Traditional Set				

SPECIALS	LEVEL/AGE	# DANCERS	COMMENTS	RESULTS

TEAMS	LEVEL/AGE	# TEAMS	COMMENTS	RESULTS

Notes:

Feis Name: _____

Date: *Location:*   *Dancer #:*

COMPETITION	LEVEL/AGE	# DANCERS	COMMENTS	RESULTS
Reel				
Light Jig				
Slip Jig				
Single Jig				
Treble Jig				
Hornpipe				
Traditional Set				

SPECIALS	LEVEL/AGE	# DANCERS	COMMENTS	RESULTS

TEAMS	LEVEL/AGE	# TEAMS	COMMENTS	RESULTS

Notes:

Feis Name: _____

Date: Location: Dancer #:

COMPETITION	LEVEL/AGE	# DANCERS	COMMENTS	RESULTS
Reel				
Light Jig				
Slip Jig				
Single Jig				
Treble Jig				
Hornpipe				
Traditional Set				

SPECIALS	LEVEL/AGE	# DANCERS	COMMENTS	RESULTS

TEAMS	LEVEL/AGE	# TEAMS	COMMENTS	RESULTS

Notes:

Feis Name: _____

Date: Location: Dancer #:

COMPETITION	LEVEL/AGE	# DANCERS	COMMENTS	RESULTS
Reel				
Light Jig				
Slip Jig				
Single Jig				
Treble Jig				
Hornpipe				
Traditional Set				

SPECIALS	LEVEL/AGE	# DANCERS	COMMENTS	RESULTS

TEAMS	LEVEL/AGE	# TEAMS	COMMENTS	RESULTS

Notes:

Feis Name: _____

Date: _____   Location: _____   Dancer #: _____

COMPETITION	LEVEL/AGE	# DANCERS	COMMENTS	RESULTS
Reel				
Light Jig				
Slip Jig				
Single Jig				
Treble Jig				
Hornpipe				
Traditional Set				

SPECIALS	LEVEL/AGE	# DANCERS	COMMENTS	RESULTS

TEAMS	LEVEL/AGE	# TEAMS	COMMENTS	RESULTS

Notes:

eis Name: _____

Date: Location: Dancer #:

COMPETITION	LEVEL/AGE	# DANCERS	COMMENTS	RESULTS
Reel				
Light Jig				
Slip Jig				
Single Jig				
Treble Jig				
Hornpipe				
Traditional Set				

SPECIALS	LEVEL/AGE	# DANCERS	COMMENTS	RESULTS

TEAMS	LEVEL/AGE	# TEAMS	COMMENTS	RESULTS

Notes:

eis Name: _____

Date: *Location:*   *Dancer #:*

COMPETITION	LEVEL/AGE	# DANCERS	COMMENTS	RESULTS
Reel				
Light Jig				
Slip Jig				
Single Jig				
Treble Jig				
Hornpipe				
Traditional Set				

SPECIALS	LEVEL/AGE	# DANCERS	COMMENTS	RESULTS

TEAMS	LEVEL/AGE	# TEAMS	COMMENTS	RESULTS

Notes:

Feis Name: _____

Date: Location: Dancer #:

COMPETITION	LEVEL/AGE	# DANCERS	COMMENTS	RESULTS
Reel				
Light Jig				
Slip Jig				
Single Jig				
Treble Jig				
Hornpipe				
Traditional Set				

SPECIALS	LEVEL/AGE	# DANCERS	COMMENTS	RESULTS

TEAMS	LEVEL/AGE	# TEAMS	COMMENTS	RESULTS

Notes:

eis Name: _____

Date: *Location:*   *Dancer #:*

COMPETITION	LEVEL/AGE	# DANCERS	COMMENTS	RESULTS
Reel				
Light Jig				
Slip Jig				
Single Jig				
Treble Jig				
Hornpipe				
Traditional Set				

SPECIALS	LEVEL/AGE	# DANCERS	COMMENTS	RESULTS

TEAMS	LEVEL/AGE	# TEAMS	COMMENTS	RESULTS

Notes:

Feis Name: _____

Date: Location: Dancer #:

COMPETITION	LEVEL/AGE	# DANCERS	COMMENTS	RESULTS
Reel				
Light Jig				
Slip Jig				
Single Jig				
Treble Jig				
Hornpipe				
Traditional Set				

SPECIALS	LEVEL/AGE	# DANCERS	COMMENTS	RESULTS

TEAMS	LEVEL/AGE	# TEAMS	COMMENTS	RESULTS

Notes:

Feis Name: _____

Date: Location: Dancer #:

COMPETITION	LEVEL/AGE	# DANCERS	COMMENTS	RESULTS
Reel				
Light Jig				
Slip Jig				
Single Jig				
Treble Jig				
Hornpipe				
Traditional Set				

SPECIALS	LEVEL/AGE	# DANCERS	COMMENTS	RESULTS

TEAMS	LEVEL/AGE	# TEAMS	COMMENTS	RESULTS

Notes:

eis Name: _____

Date: *Location:*   *Dancer #:*

COMPETITION	LEVEL/AGE	# DANCERS	COMMENTS	RESULTS
Reel				
Light Jig				
Slip Jig				
Single Jig				
Treble Jig				
Hornpipe				
Traditional Set				

SPECIALS	LEVEL/AGE	# DANCERS	COMMENTS	RESULTS

TEAMS	LEVEL/AGE	# TEAMS	COMMENTS	RESULTS

Notes:

eis Name: _____

Date: *Location:*   *Dancer #:*

COMPETITION	LEVEL/AGE	# DANCERS	COMMENTS	RESULTS
Reel				
Light Jig				
Slip Jig				
Single Jig				
Treble Jig				
Hornpipe				
Traditional Set				

SPECIALS	LEVEL/AGE	# DANCERS	COMMENTS	RESULTS

TEAMS	LEVEL/AGE	# TEAMS	COMMENTS	RESULTS

Notes:

eis Name: _____

Date: *Location:*   *Dancer #:*

COMPETITION	LEVEL/AGE	# DANCERS	COMMENTS	RESULTS
Reel				
Light Jig				
Slip Jig				
Single Jig				
Treble Jig				
Hornpipe				
Traditional Set				

SPECIALS	LEVEL/AGE	# DANCERS	COMMENTS	RESULTS

TEAMS	LEVEL/AGE	# TEAMS	COMMENTS	RESULTS

Notes:

Feis Name: _____

Date: Location: Dancer #:

COMPETITION	LEVEL/AGE	# DANCERS	COMMENTS	RESULTS
Reel				
Light Jig				
Slip Jig				
Single Jig				
Treble Jig				
Hornpipe				
Traditional Set				

SPECIALS	LEVEL/AGE	# DANCERS	COMMENTS	RESULTS

TEAMS	LEVEL/AGE	# TEAMS	COMMENTS	RESULTS

Notes:

eis Name: _____

Date: *Location:*   *Dancer #:*

COMPETITION	LEVEL/AGE	# DANCERS	COMMENTS	RESULTS
Reel				
Light Jig				
Slip Jig				
Single Jig				
Treble Jig				
Hornpipe				
Traditional Set				

SPECIALS	LEVEL/AGE	# DANCERS	COMMENTS	RESULTS

TEAMS	LEVEL/AGE	# TEAMS	COMMENTS	RESULTS

Notes:

eis Name: _____

Date: *Location:*   *Dancer #:*

COMPETITION	LEVEL/AGE	# DANCERS	COMMENTS	RESULTS
Reel				
Light Jig				
Slip Jig				
Single Jig				
Treble Jig				
Hornpipe				
Traditional Set				

SPECIALS	LEVEL/AGE	# DANCERS	COMMENTS	RESULTS

TEAMS	LEVEL/AGE	# TEAMS	COMMENTS	RESULTS

Notes:

eis Name: _____

Date: *Location:*   *Dancer #:*

COMPETITION	LEVEL/AGE	# DANCERS	COMMENTS	RESULTS
Reel				
Light Jig				
Slip Jig				
Single Jig				
Treble Jig				
Hornpipe				
Traditional Set				

SPECIALS	LEVEL/AGE	# DANCERS	COMMENTS	RESULTS

TEAMS	LEVEL/AGE	# TEAMS	COMMENTS	RESULTS

Notes:

Feis Name: _____

Date: *Location:*   *Dancer #:*

COMPETITION	LEVEL/AGE	# DANCERS	COMMENTS	RESULTS
Reel				
Light Jig				
Slip Jig				
Single Jig				
Treble Jig				
Hornpipe				
Traditional Set				

SPECIALS	LEVEL/AGE	# DANCERS	COMMENTS	RESULTS

TEAMS	LEVEL/AGE	# TEAMS	COMMENTS	RESULTS

Notes:

eis Name: _____

Date: *Location:*   *Dancer #:*

COMPETITION	LEVEL/AGE	# DANCERS	COMMENTS	RESULTS
Reel				
Light Jig				
Slip Jig				
Single Jig				
Treble Jig				
Hornpipe				
Traditional Set				

SPECIALS	LEVEL/AGE	# DANCERS	COMMENTS	RESULTS

TEAMS	LEVEL/AGE	# TEAMS	COMMENTS	RESULTS

Notes:

Feis Name: _____

Date: *Location:*   *Dancer #:*

COMPETITION	LEVEL/AGE	# DANCERS	COMMENTS	RESULTS
Reel				
Light Jig				
Slip Jig				
Single Jig				
Treble Jig				
Hornpipe				
Traditional Set				

SPECIALS	LEVEL/AGE	# DANCERS	COMMENTS	RESULTS

TEAMS	LEVEL/AGE	# TEAMS	COMMENTS	RESULTS

Notes:

Feis Name: _____

Date: Location: Dancer #:

COMPETITION	LEVEL/AGE	# DANCERS	COMMENTS	RESULTS
Reel				
Light Jig				
Slip Jig				
Single Jig				
Treble Jig				
Hornpipe				
Traditional Set				

SPECIALS	LEVEL/AGE	# DANCERS	COMMENTS	RESULTS

TEAMS	LEVEL/AGE	# TEAMS	COMMENTS	RESULTS

Notes:

Feis Name: _____

Date: Location: Dancer #:

COMPETITION	LEVEL/AGE	# DANCERS	COMMENTS	RESULTS
Reel				
Light Jig				
Slip Jig				
Single Jig				
Treble Jig				
Hornpipe				
Traditional Set				

SPECIALS	LEVEL/AGE	# DANCERS	COMMENTS	RESULTS

TEAMS	LEVEL/AGE	# TEAMS	COMMENTS	RESULTS

Notes:

Feis Name: _____

Date: Location: Dancer #:

COMPETITION	LEVEL/AGE	# DANCERS	COMMENTS	RESULTS
Reel				
Light Jig				
Slip Jig				
Single Jig				
Treble Jig				
Hornpipe				
Traditional Set				

SPECIALS	LEVEL/AGE	# DANCERS	COMMENTS	RESULTS

TEAMS	LEVEL/AGE	# TEAMS	COMMENTS	RESULTS

Notes:

eis Name: _____

Date: Location: Dancer #:

COMPETITION	LEVEL/AGE	# DANCERS	COMMENTS	RESULTS
Reel				
Light Jig				
Slip Jig				
Single Jig				
Treble Jig				
Hornpipe				
Traditional Set				

SPECIALS	LEVEL/AGE	# DANCERS	COMMENTS	RESULTS

TEAMS	LEVEL/AGE	# TEAMS	COMMENTS	RESULTS

Notes:

Feis Name: _____

Date: *Location:*   *Dancer #:*

COMPETITION	LEVEL/AGE	# DANCERS	COMMENTS	RESULTS
Reel				
Light Jig				
Slip Jig				
Single Jig				
Treble Jig				
Hornpipe				
Traditional Set				

SPECIALS	LEVEL/AGE	# DANCERS	COMMENTS	RESULTS

TEAMS	LEVEL/AGE	# TEAMS	COMMENTS	RESULTS

Notes:

Feis Name: _____

Date: Location: Dancer #:

COMPETITION	LEVEL/AGE	# DANCERS	COMMENTS	RESULTS
Reel				
Light Jig				
Slip Jig				
Single Jig				
Treble Jig				
Hornpipe				
Traditional Set				

SPECIALS	LEVEL/AGE	# DANCERS	COMMENTS	RESULTS

TEAMS	LEVEL/AGE	# TEAMS	COMMENTS	RESULTS

Notes:

Feis Name: _____

Date: Location: Dancer #:

COMPETITION	LEVEL/AGE	# DANCERS	COMMENTS	RESULTS
Reel				
Light Jig				
Slip Jig				
Single Jig				
Treble Jig				
Hornpipe				
Traditional Set				

SPECIALS	LEVEL/AGE	# DANCERS	COMMENTS	RESULTS

TEAMS	LEVEL/AGE	# TEAMS	COMMENTS	RESULTS

Notes:

eis Name: _____

Date: *Location:*   *Dancer #:*

COMPETITION	LEVEL/AGE	# DANCERS	COMMENTS	RESULTS
Reel				
Light Jig				
Slip Jig				
Single Jig				
Treble Jig				
Hornpipe				
Traditional Set				

SPECIALS	LEVEL/AGE	# DANCERS	COMMENTS	RESULTS

TEAMS	LEVEL/AGE	# TEAMS	COMMENTS	RESULTS

Notes:

Feis Name: _____

Date: Location: Dancer #:

COMPETITION	LEVEL/AGE	# DANCERS	COMMENTS	RESULTS
Reel				
Light Jig				
Slip Jig				
Single Jig				
Treble Jig				
Hornpipe				
Traditional Set				

SPECIALS	LEVEL/AGE	# DANCERS	COMMENTS	RESULTS

TEAMS	LEVEL/AGE	# TEAMS	COMMENTS	RESULTS

Notes:

eis Name: _____

Date: *Location:*   *Dancer #:*

COMPETITION	LEVEL/AGE	# DANCERS	COMMENTS	RESULTS
Reel				
Light Jig				
Slip Jig				
Single Jig				
Treble Jig				
Hornpipe				
Traditional Set				

SPECIALS	LEVEL/AGE	# DANCERS	COMMENTS	RESULTS

TEAMS	LEVEL/AGE	# TEAMS	COMMENTS	RESULTS

Notes:

eis Name: _____

Date: *Location:*   *Dancer #:*

COMPETITION	LEVEL/AGE	# DANCERS	COMMENTS	RESULTS
Reel				
Light Jig				
Slip Jig				
Single Jig				
Treble Jig				
Hornpipe				
Traditional Set				

SPECIALS	LEVEL/AGE	# DANCERS	COMMENTS	RESULTS

TEAMS	LEVEL/AGE	# TEAMS	COMMENTS	RESULTS

Notes:

Feis Name: _____

Date: Location: Dancer #:

COMPETITION	LEVEL/AGE	# DANCERS	COMMENTS	RESULTS
Reel				
Light Jig				
Slip Jig				
Single Jig				
Treble Jig				
Hornpipe				
Traditional Set				

SPECIALS	LEVEL/AGE	# DANCERS	COMMENTS	RESULTS

TEAMS	LEVEL/AGE	# TEAMS	COMMENTS	RESULTS

Notes:

Feis Name: _____

Date: *Location:*   *Dancer #:*

COMPETITION	LEVEL/AGE	# DANCERS	COMMENTS	RESULTS
Reel				
Light Jig				
Slip Jig				
Single Jig				
Treble Jig				
Hornpipe				
Traditional Set				

SPECIALS	LEVEL/AGE	# DANCERS	COMMENTS	RESULTS

TEAMS	LEVEL/AGE	# TEAMS	COMMENTS	RESULTS

Notes:

Feis Name: _____

Date: Location: Dancer #:

COMPETITION	LEVEL/AGE	# DANCERS	COMMENTS	RESULTS
Reel				
Light Jig				
Slip Jig				
Single Jig				
Treble Jig				
Hornpipe				
Traditional Set				

SPECIALS	LEVEL/AGE	# DANCERS	COMMENTS	RESULTS

TEAMS	LEVEL/AGE	# TEAMS	COMMENTS	RESULTS

Notes:

Feis Name: _____

Date: Location: Dancer #:

COMPETITION	LEVEL/AGE	# DANCERS	COMMENTS	RESULTS
Reel				
Light Jig				
Slip Jig				
Single Jig				
Treble Jig				
Hornpipe				
Traditional Set				

SPECIALS	LEVEL/AGE	# DANCERS	COMMENTS	RESULTS

TEAMS	LEVEL/AGE	# TEAMS	COMMENTS	RESULTS

Notes:

Feis Name: _____

Date: Location: Dancer #:

COMPETITION	LEVEL/AGE	# DANCERS	COMMENTS	RESULTS
Reel				
Light Jig				
Slip Jig				
Single Jig				
Treble Jig				
Hornpipe				
Traditional Set				

SPECIALS	LEVEL/AGE	# DANCERS	COMMENTS	RESULTS

TEAMS	LEVEL/AGE	# TEAMS	COMMENTS	RESULTS

Notes:

eis Name: _____

Date: *Location:*   *Dancer #:*

COMPETITION	LEVEL/AGE	# DANCERS	COMMENTS	RESULTS
Reel				
Light Jig				
Slip Jig				
Single Jig				
Treble Jig				
Hornpipe				
Traditional Set				

SPECIALS	LEVEL/AGE	# DANCERS	COMMENTS	RESULTS

TEAMS	LEVEL/AGE	# TEAMS	COMMENTS	RESULTS

Notes:

Feis Name: _____

Date: Location: Dancer #:

COMPETITION	LEVEL/AGE	# DANCERS	COMMENTS	RESULTS
Reel				
Light Jig				
Slip Jig				
Single Jig				
Treble Jig				
Hornpipe				
Traditional Set				

SPECIALS	LEVEL/AGE	# DANCERS	COMMENTS	RESULTS

TEAMS	LEVEL/AGE	# TEAMS	COMMENTS	RESULTS

Notes:

Feis Name: _____

Date: Location: Dancer #:

COMPETITION	LEVEL/AGE	# DANCERS	COMMENTS	RESULTS
Reel				
Light Jig				
Slip Jig				
Single Jig				
Treble Jig				
Hornpipe				
Traditional Set				

SPECIALS	LEVEL/AGE	# DANCERS	COMMENTS	RESULTS

TEAMS	LEVEL/AGE	# TEAMS	COMMENTS	RESULTS

travel notes

travel notes

travel notes

travel notes

Ireland

Atlantic
Ocean

Lifford • *Northern Ireland*

North Channel

• Monaghan

Sligo

Castlebar

Drogheda

Irish Sea

DUBLIN ★

Galway

Tullamore

ARAN ISLANDS

Wicklow

Arklow

Shannon
• Limerick

New Ross

Killarney
Cork

Waterford

▲
Carrauntoohil

Celtic Sea

Made in the USA
Middletown, DE
02 January 2024

47083222R00062